Frog's Diary

If found, please return this diary to:

NAME	Frog
ADDRESS	The Pond
AGE	5 years old
COLOURING	Mottled green

Favourite Things:

FOOD	Flies, slugs and beetles
PLACES	Cool, muddy places
TIME OF YEAR	Spring

Published by Victoria House Publishing Ltd. A Division of The Reader's Digest Children's Books
King's Court, Parsonage Lane, Bath BA1 1ER

Conceived, edited and designed by Tucker Slingsby Limited
Berkeley House, 73 Upper Richmond Road, London SW15 2SZ

Copyright © 1999 Tucker Slingsby Ltd.

ISBN 1-84088-0546

Illustrations by Robert Morton, Robin Carter and Philip Bishop
Text by Steve Parker

Frog's Diary

with the help of
Steve Parker

·······

Reader's Digest
Children's Books

ALL ABOUT ME

Well here we go — the first page
of my very own diary. I've always
wanted to keep one and this year
I'm going to do it. I'll call it 'A Year
in the Life of an Observant Frog'!

I'm feeling pretty stiff and slow
today. I'm also very hungry! It's not
surprising really, as I've been asleep
for — well, months! The whole
of Winter in fact.

It's still not very warm yet
and I'm not at my speediest
when it's cold. So I'll just do
a few stretching exercises
today. I can look for food
tomorrow, when I'm warmer
and can move more quickly.

ME - EATING A
TASTY SNACK

MY POND - THAT'S ME
ON THE LILY PAD!

| January | February | March | April | May | June |

I think I should start this diary with a few notes about me. I'm a frog. I've got two big eyes to see my food and one wide mouth to gulp it down. I've got a tubby green body, two strong back legs for leaping with, and two small front legs for landing on — but no tail. Know-all Newt told me I'm an ~~amfibian~~ amphibian. He gave me this bit of paper out of a book to explain what this means. He's one too!

When it's warm enough, I live in the Pond. It's very busy. There are ducks, fish and bugs, as well as lots of other frogs, and visitors from far away. Life is never dull. There's always someone to catch for lunch!

MY DRAWING OF NEWT

All About Amphibians
(say it 'am-fibb-ee-ans')

- Amphibians are one of the main groups of vertebrates – animals with backbones. The others are fish, reptiles, birds and mammals.
- There are about 4,000 kinds, or species, of amphibians.
- Amphibians live all around the world, except for cold polar lands or in the sea. Most prefer lakes, streams and damp places. But some like deserts!
- Amphibians are cold-blooded. This means that their bodies are the same temperature as their surroundings. Cold weather makes them too cool to move. Warm weather lets them be active.
- There are three main groups of amphibians:

1 Newts and salamanders
They have tails.

2 Frogs and toads
They don't have tails.

3 Caecilians
They don't have tails or legs. They look like big earthworms and live mainly in the soil of tropical forests.

HOORAY! IT'S SPRING

At last! Sunshine in my Den. This is where I sleep all Winter. Newt says our Winter sleep is called hibernation. All I know is that I'm too cold to move anywhere. Now I'm warming up. Tomorrow I plan to hop over the log, across the bog, over the road (the dangerous bit) and on to my favourite place — the Pond. Newt's coming too.

I'm STARVING. After all, I haven't eaten for five months! I can't waste time looking for food here so I'll have to gulp down a meal or two on the ~~jurney jorney~~ way.

DRAWINGS OF WHAT I WANT TO EAT TOMORROW!

BEETLES — crunchy outside, soft and tasty inside. Yum, yum!

SLUGS — slow and slippery. They slide down easily!

I picked this snowdrop to show that Spring is almost here. But it's no good to eat!

| January | February | March | April | May | June |

July   August   September   October   November   December

BACK TO THE POND

The journey to the Pond took ages — two days in fact! I'm small and slow, and I have to keep hiding from creatures that want to **EAT ME**! And I have to shelter from the sun which can dry me out.

First I waddled along, then had a rest. After a small hop or two more, it was time to rest again. It would be quicker if I took big leaps but they're terribly tiring! Leaps are great for escaping from danger but no good for a long journey like this.

I had to watch out for danger every hop of the way. Then, just after one long waddle and a small hop, I took a pause. Or should I say **PAWS**! There in front of me was Cat! I took one big leap, and another and — phew, I was back at my pond with my friends! Was I glad **THAT** was all over.

It was good to see the usual crowd at the Pond. Some of them, like Toad, are slow like me. But Duck, Mouse — and of course horrible Cat — move much faster. They always seem to be warm. It must be in their blood. Newt calls them warm-blooded.

OOPS — MUDDY FOOT!

MY AMAZING LEAP AWAY FROM DANGER!

BY FROG

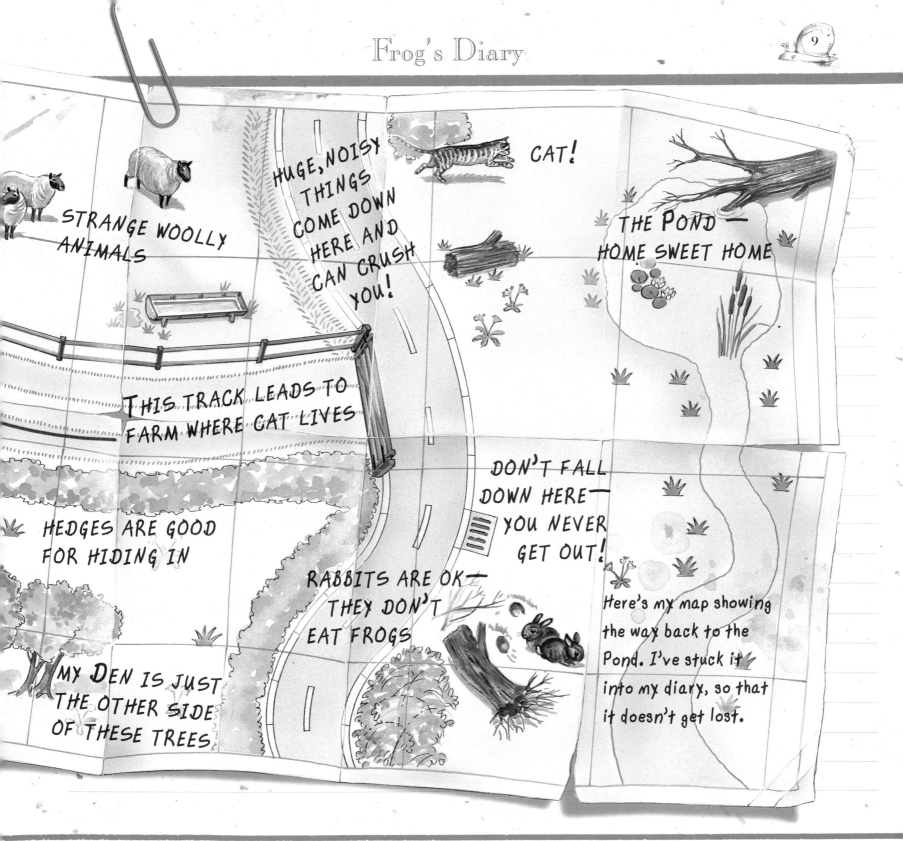

STRANGE WOOLLY ANIMALS

HUGE, NOISY THINGS COME DOWN HERE AND CAN CRUSH YOU!

CAT!

THE POND — HOME SWEET HOME

THIS TRACK LEADS TO FARM WHERE CAT LIVES

DON'T FALL DOWN HERE — YOU NEVER GET OUT!

HEDGES ARE GOOD FOR HIDING IN

RABBITS ARE OK — THEY DON'T EAT FROGS

MY DEN IS JUST THE OTHER SIDE OF THESE TREES

Here's my map showing the way back to the Pond. I've stuck it into my diary, so that it doesn't get lost.

HOME SWEET HOME

The Pond is **PERFECT.** There's lots of lovely wet water to swim in and to keep my skin nice and moist. The banks are marvellously muddy and damp. The plants are big enough to give me shade and to hide in. And there are lots of small creatures to catch and eat. **YUMMY!**

Best of all — there are lots of other frogs. For most of the year I keep myself to myself, but in the Spring we frogs all get together to ~~bread~~ breed.

As soon as I had found a comfortable muddy spot, I checked out the Pond for danger. *I* **ALWAYS** do that! The Pond looked fine — full of cool, clear water, not murky and almost dried out, like last year. But on the bank were the tracks of a strange animal...

MY DRAWING OF 'THE STRANGE FOOTPRINT'

| January | February | March | April | May | June |

STRANGE TRACKS

I have to be a bit of a nature detective to survive! Animals walk across the soft mud and leave footprints behind. Some tracks don't worry me — like Squirrel and Deer. Others, especially Gull, Badger and Heron, spell **DANGER.**

I've never seen anything like the footprints left in the mud today. I thought this page — from a book I found by the Pond — would help, but the stranger's feet aren't in there.

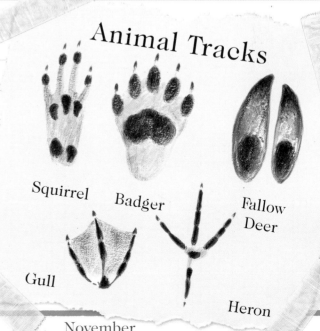

Animal Tracks

Squirrel Badger Fallow Deer

Gull

Heron

WURP, RIBBIT, CROAK!

What a noisy few days it's been! My froggy friends are swimming and splashing, calling and croaking. It's always like this in the early Spring because it's our breeding season.

All the male frogs, including me, began croaking and calling to the female frogs. We make our loud croaks by sucking air in and blowing it out. This makes our chins swell up like BALLOONS!

When the females heard the noise, they joined us in the Pond. Frogs don't have big, sticky-out ears like Rabbits but our eardrums work just as well. Anyway, we made so much noise, the females couldn't miss it!

Then we all pushed and shoved, trying to find the best-looking partner. Eventually everyone finds a mate. Each male frog holds on to the female, sometimes for two or three days!

January   February   March   April   May   June

The females lay their eggs in the water. Each egg is a tiny black dot covered in jelly. The males then lay their sperm over the eggs.

I don't really understand this part but Know-all Newt says that each egg has to join with a sperm, before it can grow into a baby frog. Newt calls this 'fertilization'.

All I know is that the Pond is absolutely packed with slippery, jelly-covered eggs. Even I know this is called frog-spawn!

THAT'S ME — CROAKING AT THE TOP OF MY VOICE!

July   August   September   October   November   December

Frog's Diary

January   February   March   April   May   June

MY SPECIAL JELLYBABIES!

Today, I fell out with Newt. He's an **EGG-STEALER**! Newt thinks frog-spawn is a tasty snack, so do some of the other animals in the Pond. Water beetles, dragonfly nymphs and fish all help themselves to our eggs!

I expect frogs' eggs are very tasty but to eat them seems awful! Of course, frogs lay lots of eggs, so perhaps it doesn't matter too much if some get stolen.

Each female frog can lay about 2,000 eggs in a big clump. Toads lay about the same number, but in a long rope of jelly, like a necklace, wound around underwater leaves and stems. Newt's own eggs are a bit like ours, but smaller. And each one is laid separately, usually under a leaf.

Thinking about it — the Pond would be terribly crowded if all the eggs hatched. Perhaps it's just as well so many get eaten!

I've noticed that different animals have very different eggs. Here are ~~my obcervashuns~~ the things I've spotted:

• Pond-snail's eggs are like ours, covered in jelly. But they are **MUCH** smaller, and laid in a strip on an underwater leaf.

• Moorhen's eggs are huge! They have a hard outside shell instead of jelly. Which is just as well, since they are **NOT IN WATER** at all! They're outside, in the air. Without a hard shell, they'd dry up and shrivel.

• All the birds seem to lay hard-shelled eggs. Sometimes the empty shells fall into the water from their nests.

THIS IS MOORHEN

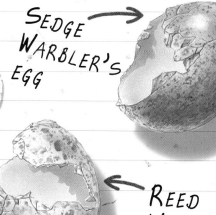

SEDGE WARBLER'S EGG

REED WARBLER'S EGG

MOORHEN'S EGG

LITTLE WRIGGLERS

It's now the middle of Spring and I've been too busy to write my diary for a while. Every day is warmer — and more crowded! Our eggs have hatched into tiny tadpoles — I call them wrigglers because that's just what they do!

Dotty babies

This picture shows the tiny frog babies before they hatched. They floated about in their jelly for around two weeks, before wriggling free. I like them at this stage. They're no trouble! But hungry fish (and newts!) are a problem...

Little squirmers

As soon as they've hatched, the little rascals eat almost anything they can find — even bits of rotting plants and animals. They're funny-looking little things with a tail and no legs. Just the opposite of me!

Tadpole Timetable

Week 1   2,000 eggs
Week 3   1,000 baby tadpoles hatched
Week 5   Less than 500 tadpoles left — many are eaten by pond creatures and birds
Week 7   200 tadpoles with back legs
Week 10 100 tadpoles with their tails starting to shrink
Week 12 25 tadpoles have survived and now have front legs too
Week 15 Only 10 left – no longer tadpoles, they have become froglets

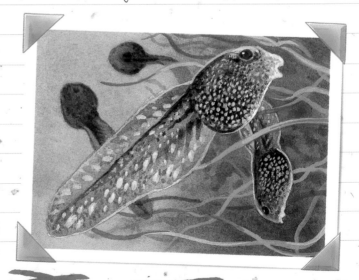

January   February   March   April   May   June

Time for legs

About seven weeks after hatching, the babies start to grow back legs and learn to swim by kicking them in the water. I call it the froggy-paddle!

More legs and less tail!

About five weeks after the froggy-paddle stage, the tadpoles' front legs pop out and their tails began to shrink. There's no stopping them now — they can breathe out of water by gulping air into their lungs. They want to start jumping out of the pond!

My favourite Froglet

This is a favourite daughter of mine — 15 weeks after hatching. To look at her now, sitting on MY lily pad, you'd never guess she'd started as an egg and been a wriggly little tadpole. Newt, who knows long words (and how to spell them), says that this change in shape is called 'metamorphosis'. All frogs (and newts) do it!

I'M HUNGRY

Whrrrr. A big – and I mean **BIG** – dragonfly whizzed past me today and landed on a leaf. I was hungry, and dragonflies are very tasty. Some are so big that if I catch them, I don't have to eat again for days! But they're strong, too. They can give you nasty jabs with their mouth and the sharp claws on their feet.

I catch small flies by ~~fliking~~ flicking out my tongue and **SNAP** — they're stuck on its sticky tip. This monster looked too big for that, so I went for a bold approach. I leapt up and grabbed it in my — though I say it myself — fabulously wide mouth.

I had a bit of a struggle to swallow the dragonfly but it was worth the effort. It was the best meal I've had for a long time.

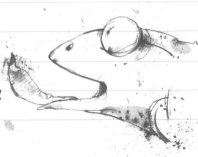

THIS IS MY DRAWING OF MY BIG, STICKY TONGUE!

Fast food . . .

I only eat living, moving animals. Nothing dead — **UGH!** Butterflies are pretty — pretty tasty!

Flies are yummy but bees make a nice change. Bees get busy in a flower and don't notice me creeping up!

. . . and slow food!

Snails are terrific! So slow and so easy to catch! I crunch them up and spit out the bits of shell.

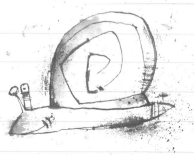

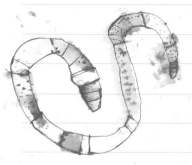

Frogs don't have teeth so we swallow worms whole. They wriggle all the way down. Yummy!

July   August   September   October   November   December

THE SCARY PART

Today was a **BAD DAY**! Heron visited our Pond. I haven't been so frightened since I saw Fox last Winter. Sitting at the edge of the Pond, I felt strange ripples in the water. I dived away just in time. A huge foot landed **EXACTLY** where I had been sitting!

I kept very still. My mottled green skin matches the mud and stones, so if I don't move, I'm almost invisible. Well, at least I've survived five Winters!

Nothing happened for a long time. A few other pond animals began to move about. But I could still see the shadow of that big leg, so I stayed **VERY, VERY STILL.** Then suddenly, **SPLASH!** A great, sharp beak stabbed through the water. It was absolutely terrifying. That beak was bigger than me!

A FEATHER HERON LEFT BEHIND

It was Heron! I actually saw his head and his big, beady eyes. He grabbed a fish in his beak, pulled it high into the air and, GULP! The water swirled, the great bird flapped his wings and was gone. The danger was over.

Many creatures try to eat us frogs. We have to watch out for lots of birds. Herons are the greediest, then there are gulls and grebes by the Pond, and crows and magpies hopping along the banks. I've seen frogs caught by cats, rats, foxes, hedgehogs and grass snakes. I hate cats the most — they watch us for hours and then slash their sharp claws through the water. UGH!

Daily Clarion

Vanishing Pond Life

If you value the frogs, newts and fish in your pond, cover it with a net! Frogs and other water creatures are being caught and killed at an alarming rate. Herons are often blamed for emptying a pond, but your cat may be the real culprit.

SUMMER NIGHTS

I don't do much during the long summer days. I have a 'see-food' diet. If I see food, I eat it! Otherwise, I just sit around and relax. Some animals are so busy, rushing here and there, always doing something. It makes me tired just to watch them.

During the night, I do even less. Darkness is so-oo-oo spooky! I just gaze, stare and watch. By day, my huge eyes can spot tiny gnats and midges flitting past. But at night, I can't see very well. So I find a safe place, sit tight, and wait until daylight. If the Moon is bright, I can see animals moving around. Last night was lovely and warm, so I recorded the events.

MOTHS LIKE THIS ARE ALWAYS FLITTING ABOUT AT NIGHT

NATURE NOTES - BY FROG

Written by the light of Glow-worm and her friends. (They're not really worms, more a kind of beetle. They glow to attract a mate. I've stuck in a picture to show what they look like.)

SKY - Bat is flitting about. Bat is like a bird, but has fur instead of feathers. Bat is always chasing Moth. Why? Maybe to catch and eat, like I catch Fly.

NEAR - After catching a caterpillar, I swallowed it whole. I saw Mouse eat one too — there must be a shortage of her usual seeds, nuts and berries. Land-snail slowly slides up a stem, looking for juicy leaves to eat. Snails certainly live life in the slow lane!

FAR - In the distant field, I can just see Deer nibbling at leaves. I know Deer because she comes to the Pond to drink, and leaves her footprints in the mud.

OH NO! THERE'S WEASEL! Mouse is in serious danger. But a really hungry Weasel might even eat me! Time to hide...

Why do Glow-worms glow?
Glow-worms have two substances in their bodies that produce light when they react with the oxygen in the air.

FEMALE

MALE

July   August   September   October   November   December

DRY AND DANGEROUS

PHEW, IT'S HOT! I may be cold-blooded, but today, I'm sure my blood is hotter than Mouse's! I can only stay in the sun for a few minutes before my skin starts to feel dry and stiff. If I don't hide in the water or under a cool, damp stone I could dry out and **DIE!**

The Pond always gets smaller in Summer when the Sun's hot and high in the sky. But this year, it's much worse than usual. It hasn't rained for **WEEKS.**

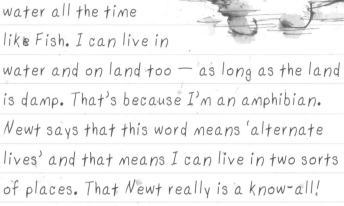

Luckily I don't have to live in water all the time like Fish. I can live in water and on land too — as long as the land is damp. That's because I'm an amphibian. Newt says that this word means 'alternate lives' and that means I can live in two sorts of places. That Newt really is a know-all!

In fact, my friends and I don't stay in the Pond for long. We go there in early Spring to breed. By early Summer, we usually move to nearby patches of damp undergrowth, bushes and shady plants. Our amphibian cousins, Toad and Newt, do the same.

If it doesn't rain soon the Pond will disappear completely and so will Fish and his friends.

LOVELY LILY PADS ! GREAT TO SIT ON — OR HIDE UNDER LIKE A SUNSHADE

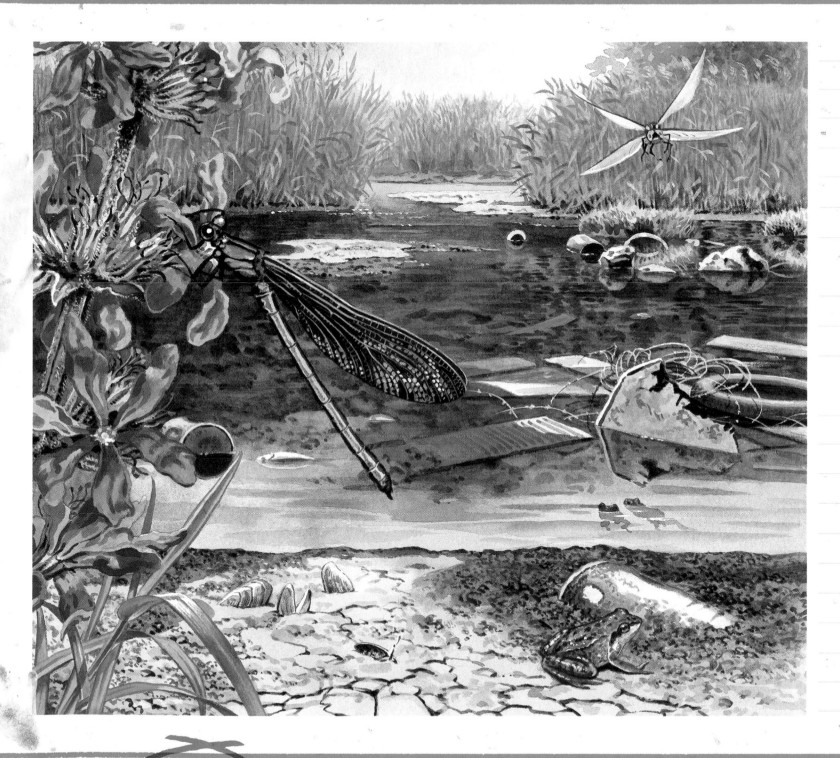

July   August   September   October   November   December

TIME TO LEAVE

Today Summer has turned to Autumn. The sun is weaker, days are shorter, clouds are lower, raindrops are bigger. It's good to feel the rain, but it's a bit chilly. It cools my body down and I can't move as quickly.

The rains have filled up the Pond and everywhere's lovely and damp. I like wet grass and leaves but Sparrow and Shrew are shivering. There aren't many flies and other things for me to catch. They must go away for Winter too.

Everything's changing. Leaves are turning brown and falling off the trees. Seeds, berries and nuts grow in their place. Mouse and Vole love them. I tried a blackberry once. YUCK! It didn't wriggle, and it didn't taste of meat. Frogs are NOT vegetarians!

NOW ONE'S FALLEN ON MY PAGE! WHAT A MESS!

It will soon be time for my winter sleep. I'll turn back to my map (how useful this diary is!). It will show me the way back to my cosy Den.

Goodbye, Pond, until next year!

THINGS TO EAT ON THE WAY BACK

SPIDER has lots of wriggly legs and a hairy body, but is soft and juicy inside.

CRANEFLY is very spindly. I hardly taste the thin legs and wings, they snap off at my first bite!

BUSH CRICKET's back legs are strong and kick hard, like mine. Ouch, my mouth!

DUNG FLY I'm not sure what 'dung' is, but this fly is extra-juicy and extra-sweet. Yummy!

Back to Sleep

I nearly didn't make it back to the Den. I saw some of those strange footprints I first spotted by the Pond in Spring. Then I saw the creature who made them — MINK! She's worse than Heron. She's as bad as Cat! She can swim as well as I can, and eats water animals — fish, newts and frogs!

I hid until Mink had gone. I got almost too cold to move but I knew I had to keep going.

I reached my Den at last. It was nearly dark. I hopped along the track, through the trees and found my hidey-hole just as I left it. Thank goodness it was still there. Last year, Toad went back to her usual Winter Den, but it had gone. No trees or bushes. Just a huge, flat, smelly blackness, with giant wheels, that can crush you flat.

ACORN - A FAVOURITE WITH SQUIRREL

OAK LEAF

This is my final entry in my very first Diary. Soon I'll bury myself in leaves, moss and soil, safe from frosts and ~~preditors~~ predators. (That's another word I learned from Newt!) It's been a great year, because I've learned lots of new things and most of all, I've survived! Few frogs reach such a ripe old age. Next Spring I'll be six!

When it's warm again, I think I'll start another diary. I want to draw some more pictures too. But now it's time to settle down. I'll just take a last look at the cards and photos my relatives have sent me this year. I've stuck them in on the next page.

My Froggy Friends

These frogs are some of my friends and relations. They look different from me because they live in faraway lands.

They sometimes send me postcards, photos and letters. I always write back to them. They like to hear about life in the Pond and I do little drawings for them too!

BEADY

He's a Red-eyed Tree Frog. Pretty smart, eh? Beady lives in a warm, wet, tropical forest in Costa Rica. That's in Central America — it takes ages for his postcards to arrive! Beady's quite small, but he has huge eyes so he can see in the forest gloom. He's got suckers on his fingertips too! These grip the slippery leaves and branches. I'd like to visit Beady — a warm, damp forest sounds good to me!

SHEILA

This is my friend from Australia. She's a Water-holding Frog. She lives in a place that sounds horrible — a dry desert. **SCARY!** She hides underground for months, in a kind of wet sleeping bag made from her own body water. When it rains, she digs up to the surface. Sounds a pretty strange life to me!

January   February   March   April   May   June

GREEDY

These are my favourite snaps! Greedy's a Bush Squeaker. She sent these photos to me all the way from Africa. Greedy says Africa is very hot, with lots of flies, so she sent pictures of her catching one. (I can do that tongue trick too, of course.) Greedy says she's careful not to sunbathe too much. Dry skin can be deadly to us frogs!

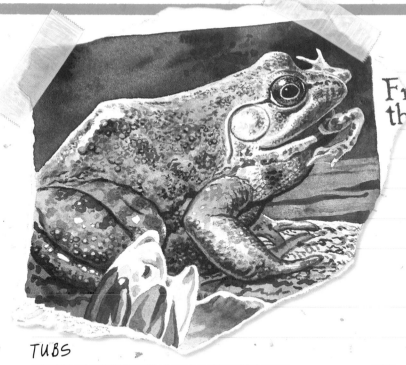

TUBS

This is one cousin I don't want to meet! Tubs is an American Bullfrog. He is one of the biggest, strongest frogs in the world. Bullfrogs eat lots of animals, including rats, lizards, snakes — even other frogs like me. **GULP!**

BLUE FROG

All frogs have skin which tastes horrible. That often stops birds from eating us. Smarty's a Koikoi Frog from South America — his skin can kill predators! He says his bright blue colours tell animals 'Don't touch'!